LOUISVILLE

The Cubby
Long Weekend Guide

TABLE OF CONTENTS

Chapter 1

WHY LOUISVILLE?

If you follow the booze industry, or even hang out in semi-fashionable bars and lounges anywhere in the world, you can't have escaped the realization that bourbon has become one of the hottest categories in the spirits business.

Kentucky is the Bourbon Capital of the World, and within the Bluegrass State, the epicenter of all this activity is Louisville. People come here before they go out into the hinterlands to visit the distilleries. (Actually, the town of Bardstown, about 40 minutes from Louisville, trademarked the term "Bourbon Capital of the World," but that's hair-splitting.)

The amount of bourbon selling each year goes up greater than any other spirit. Sales will top $5 billion shortly. Production of the liquor has jumped 50% just over the last decade.

If you added up all the barrels currently aging in Louisville distilleries, the number would be greater

LOUISVILLE

The Cubby
2024
Long Weekend Guide

No business listed in this guide has provided *anything* free to be included.

James Cubby

Fisher Collins Press

than the number of people that live in the state, and for that matter, the number of horses, *combined!*

Now, that's a lot of bourbon.

A great deal of the increase in bourbon shipments has been to foreign countries, places like Dubai, Singapore, Tokyo, where a taste for bourbon has become all the rage among the moneyed elites in these countries. The greatest growth has come within the super premium categories.

As sales have soared against other segments of the liquor industry (vodka, tequila, gin, Scotch), the so-called Big Six distilleries (including Jim Beam, Heaven Hill, Brown-Forman, Wild Turkey, Four Roses and Diageo) have ramped up production.

The new keen interest from consumers has proved strong enough to encourage numerous entrepreneurs to launch craft distilleries. And while the Big Six still gobble up sales, accounting for some 90%, there's room enough for these craft distilleries to make a dent because they tend to produce only high-end, handcrafted bourbons that are highly prized.

All these factors have led to an increase in tourism for Louisville and the rest of the state. Tourists visiting distilleries passed the 500,000 mark recently, and the numbers keep rising.

Along with all this attention, the indie foodie scene in Louisville has exploded, with great new restaurants popping up every week.

But it's not all about bourbon in Louisville. The city has a fascinating history, made even more notable by what happens the first Saturday in May.

That marks the annual running of the Kentucky Derby, of course. It was conceived in 1872 when Col. Meriwether Lewis Clark Jr. (grandson of the Lewis & Clark Expedition's William Clark) returned from a European tour having attended the English Derby and the Grand Prix de Paris at the famous racetrack Longchamp.

Once back home, he put together the Louisville Jockey Club and raised money to build a track. (The track gets its name from brothers Henry and John Churchill, who contributed the land for the track.) It's been run every year since 1875.

It's been called "The Most Exciting Two Minutes In Sports," and I've always wondered what brilliant PR guy came up with that stupendous moniker. It sounds like hype, but if you've ever seen the Kentucky Derby, you'll realize it's not hype at all. It really is the most exciting two minutes in sports. The Derby record is still held by Secretariat, who ran the race in 1:59.

The race is 1 ¼ miles long. The Derby is the first race in the Triple Crown. After the Derby, the second leg is the Preakness Stakes in Baltimore (at 1 3/16 miles), following by the Belmont Stakes (at 1 ½ miles).

The city fathers have been trying to create more of a year-round tourist city out of Louisville, and the bourbon industry seems to be aiding this goal. As I said above, the interesting food scene is helping as well.

After the Downtown area, you'll want to explore **Highlands** for its excellent shopping. This is on **Bardstown Road** (from around Broadway down to the Douglass Loop) where you'll find a wide variety of cafés, upscale restaurants, art galleries, lots of bars (some great dives as well).

You hear all kinds of weird pronunciations of the town's name. You even hear the god-awful "Lewisville," which is so wrong. Then there's *LOOey-vil* and *LOOuh-vuhl* and *LU-vuhl*.

In my opinion, the best way is: *LOOuh-vuhl*.

Chapter 2

GETTING ABOUT

You will only need a car if you venture far from Downtown, Highlands, Frankfort Avenue, Old Louisville. Everything is quite walkable. But you'll need a car to go anywhere else.

Use **Uber** or **Lyft** if you like. They can take you to the airport but will not pick you up there. (Legal hassles.) Use them to get around town if you don't want to rent a car.

There's a bus system, **TARC**, that is all right. Buses now have bike racks and there's an aggressive program to make the roads even more bike-friendly than they already are.

Get the bus schedule here - www.ridetarc.org

Chapter 3

WHERE TO STAY

21c MUSEUM HOTEL
700 West Main St, Louisville, 502-217-6300
www.21chotel.com
Located in historic downtown Louisville, this hotel
that opened in 2006 (in an area of old tobacco
warehouses that were restored) is a unique
combination of a 90-room boutique hotel with a
contemporary art museum, an award-winning locally-
sourced restaurant and a civic center.

This is a most interesting place, a destination all by itself, really, because of the "museum" aspect of the property, which commissions site-specific works and curated dynamic group and solo exhibitions, which are free to the public and open every day of the year. Owners Laura Lee Brown and Steve Wilson display not only their own art, but others' as well. By opening the place, they insure a steady stream of local customers.

With all this art around, the bar and restaurant are naturally filled with the local creative types that make Louisville so interesting. The restaurant, **Proof on Main**, was named one the Best Restaurants in the country by "Esquire." The bar here carries over 50 Kentucky bourbons.

Guest rooms and suites offer spacious accommodations and a comfortable respite from all the activity that fills the museum. Amenities include original art, 42 HDTV flat screen TVs with full cable, luxurious bedding, pewter mint julep cups, and free high-speed Wi-Fi.

BROWN HOTEL

335 West Broadway, Louisville, 888-888-5252
www.brownhotel.com
Home of the original **"Hot Brown,"** this historic
AAA Four Diamond luxury hotel (dating back to
1923) offers beautiful accommodations and boasts the
reputation as one of the finest hotels in the South. The
opulent two-story lobby greets guests with its
beautiful marble floors, hand-painted, coffered ceiling
and Palladian-style windows. The bar in the lobby is
another big local hangout. Amenities include
European goose down duvets, feather beds, flat-
screen TVs and free high-speed Internet access. The
Brown is known for its in-house restaurant, the
English Grill. Conveniently located next to the
Brown Theatre and close to the Palace Theatre, 4th
Street Live, and other local attractions.

THE DUPONT MANSION BED &

BREAKFAST 1317 South Fourth St, Louisville, 502-638-0045 www.dupontmansion.com
Located in historic Old Louisville, this beautiful B&B is one of the finest inns in Kentucky. Beautifully restored, this 1884 Italian -style inn offers only 7 guest rooms with private baths, whirlpool tubs, and the amenities of a luxury hotel. Every morning a gourmet breakfast is served in the dining room. Free refreshments are served every evening. Amenities include flat screen cable TV, electric fireplace inserts, luxury lines, and free wireless Internet service.

EMBASSY SUITES BY HILTON

9940 Corporate Campus Dry, Louisville, 502-426-9191
www.hilton.com/search/es/us/ky/louisville
This hotel offers spacious suites with separate living rooms. Amenities include complimentary cooked-to-order breakfast, flat-screen TVs, and complimentary Wi-Fi. Facility features include: an open-air atrium, indoor pool, whirlpool and fitness center.
Conveniently located to attractions like Churchill

Downs, Ox moor Mall and the Louisville Slugger
Museum.

GALT HOUSE HOTEL
140 N 4th St, Louisville, 502-589-5200
www.galthouse.com
This is the largest hotel in Louisville with 1,300 guest
rooms, including 650 suites. Amenities include Wi-Fi
(fee), flat screen HDTVs, and free shopping shuttle.
Hotel features include seasonal outdoor pool, salon,
spa, 6 restaurants and lounges, and boutiques. Free
Wi-Fi in public places. Non-smoking hotel.

**HAMPTON INN LOUISVILLE
DOWNTOWN** 101 E Jefferson St, Louisville,
502-585-2200
https://www.hilton.com/en/hotels/sdfdthx-
hampton-louisville-downtown
Modern hotel with 173 guest rooms typical of the
Hampton Inn chain. Amenities include free Wi-Fi,
flat-screen TVs, coffeemakers and free hot breakfast
and weekday breakfast bags to go. Suites have wet
bars, minifridges and microwaves. Hotel features
include fitness center, indoor pool, and business
center. Conveniently located near downtown
attractions like the Louisville Slugger Factory and the
entertainment district.

HYATT REGENCY LOUISVILLE

320 West Jefferson St, Louisville, 502-581-1234
https://www.hyatt.com/en-US/hotel/kentucky/hyatt-regency-louisville/sdfrl?src=corp_lclb_gmb_seo_sdfrl
True to the Hyatt name, this hotel offers spacious guestrooms and suites and a little dose of southern hospitality. Amenities include flat screen TVs and Wi-Fi (fee). Hotel features include: 24-hour gym, outdoor tennis court, indoor pool, on-site restaurant/bar and a bagel shop. Conveniently located near Kentucky International Convention Center (with a direct connection to the hotel).

THE INN AT WOODHAVEN

401 S Hubbards Ln, Louisville, 502-895-1011 www.innatwoodhaven.com
NEIGHBORHOOD: St. Matthews
Built in 1853, this is one of the premier inns of Kentucky. The Inn, set on a lovely tree-lined street in a restful neighborhood, offers 8 elegantly furnished guest rooms all furnished with antiques and reproductions, four-poster beds and wing armchairs. In good weather, you can sit on the spacious front.

porch and catch the breeze. Amenities:
Complimentary breakfast and Wi-Fi, flat-screen TVs,
mini-fridges, and coffeemakers. Facilities: 14-foot
ceilings and floor to ceiling diamond paned windows.
Some rooms feature whirlpool tubs, steam showers
and/or fireplaces. Conveniently located near
Louisville attractions, parks, fine dining and shopping
areas.

SEELBACH HILTON HOTEL

500 S 4th St, Louisville, 502-585-
3200 www.seelbachhilton.com
Built in 1905, it is considered a landmark to "the
golden era" with its grand ambiance that inspired
author F. Scott Fitzgerald to use the Seelbach as a
backdrop for Tom and Daisy Buchanan's wedding in
"The Great Gatsby." (The hotel even has a cameo in
the movie.) And now a recent $12 million renovation

has taken this grand old hotel and combined it with all of the contemporary necessities. So now, you can not only experience genteel, Southern hospitality in historic grandeur. You can do so in updated guestrooms with new furniture, lighting and carpet while watching 37" hi-def televisions and taking advantage of high-speed Internet access. Fitness room, business center.

STAYBRIDGE SUITES LOUISVILLE EAST
11711 Gateworth Way, Louisville, 502-244-9511
Blankenbaker Pkwy & I-64 (Exit 17)
https://www.ihg.com/staybridge/hotels/us/en/louisvill e/sdfmt/hoteldetail
This extended stay hotel offers 94 guest rooms and suites. Amenities include free continental breakfast, free Wi-Fi and cable TV. Hotel facilities include outdoor pool, fitness center, laundry facilities, and business center.
Conveniently located near attractions like Renaissance Fun Park, Churchill Downs, and Maker's Mark Distillery.

HOTEL

Chapter 4
WHERE TO EAT

610 MAGNOLIA

610 W Magnolia Ave, Louisville, 502- 636-0783
www.610magnolia.com
CUISINE: Creative Southern
DRINKS: Full Bar
SERVING: Dinner Thursday-Saturday. Verify other
days. Don't walk in. Book ahead.
PRICE RANGE: $$$$
NEIGHBORHOOD: Downtown
This is one of celebrated Chef Ed Lee's places. It's a
small room with bricked flooring and bare-topped
wooden tables. For a fine dining place, it's almost as

if they wanted to go bare bones with the décor, but it's
still quite nice with brightly colored art on the walls.
Best idea here is to go for the Tasting Menu. It'll give
you a feel for his inventive twist on Southern cooking.
Expect items like smoked octopus; pan roasted lamb
chop with shred leg of lamb; spiced catfish with bok
choy; shaved fennel; lobster medallions; chicken thigh
confit; pork osso bucco.

8UP

350 W Chestnut St, Louisville, 502-631-4180
www.8uplouisville.com/
CUISINE: American (New)
DRINKS: Full Bar
SERVING: Breakfast & Dinner
PRICE RANGE: $$
Trendy eatery featuring an eclectic menu popular
with sophisticated guests and foodies. This 90-seat
restaurant offers beautiful view of the city and an
open kitchen so you can watch your meal being
prepared. Popular nightlife spot. Open air rooftop
bar. More of a scene than a dining establishment.

BLUE DOG BAKERY & CAFÉ

2868 Frankfort Ave, Louisville, 502-899-9800
www.bluedogbakeryandcafe.com/
CUISINE: Breakfast/Cafe
DRINKS: Full bar
SERVING: Breakfast & Lunch
PRICE RANGE: $$
NEIGHBORHOOD: Crescent Hill/The Avenue
Bakery/café offering a wide range of artisanal breads,
croissants and muffins as well as delicious breakfast

and lunch. Menu favorites: Breakfast pizza and French toast. Place gets crowded so there's often a wait.

BRENDON'S CATCH 23
505 S 4th St, Louisville, 502-909-0053
www.bcatch23.com
CUISINE: Steakhouse/Seafood
DRINKS: Full Bar
SERVING: Dinner; closed Sundays
PRICE RANGE: $$$
A high-end, chef driven restaurant offering a creative menu of seafood and steaks. Menu favorites include Sea Bass & Scallops. Sophisticated dining at its best with large dining room, private dining rooms and cocktail bar known for its hand-crafted cocktails.

COALS ARTISAN PIZZA
3730 Frankfort Ave, Louisville, 502-742-8200
www.coalsartisanpizza.com

CUISINE: Pizza/Italian
DRINKS: Full Bar
SERVING: Lunch & Dinner
PRICE RANGE: $$
Here you'll find great pizza prepared in their coal-fired oven. Menu offers a great selection of pizzas with gourmet toppings and a selection of Italian classics. If you're a fan of having lots of meat on your pizza, this is the place for you. Especially savory is the Italian sausage stuffed with flavorful fennel and the spicy pepperoni. Great selection of wine and beers.

CON HUEVOS

2339 Frankfort Ave, Louisville, 502-384-3027
4938 US Hwy 42, Louisville, 502-384-3744
http://www.conhuevos.com/
CUISINE: Mexican
DRINKS: No Booze
SERVING: Breakfast & Lunch only, from 7 a.m.
PRICE RANGE: $$
NEIGHBORHOOD: 2 locations in Brownsboro
& Holiday Manor
Mexican eatery (2 locations) with a fun interior with delightfully whimsical Mexican tiled floors, brick walls painted white, a few distressed wood furniture pieces. Street-side seating in good weather. Serves only breakfast and lunch. Favorites: Dulce de Leche French toast and
Mexican breakfast. Order and pay at counter then your meal is delivered to counter or table. Serving Cuban coffee.

DOC CROWS

127 West Main St, Louisville, 502-587-1626
www.doccrows.com
CUISINE: Southern, American
DRINKS: Full Bar
SERVING: Lunch, Dinner
PRICE RANGE: $$
NEIGHBORHOOD: Downtown
Also on Whiskey Row is this locals' favorite that is in
the old Bonnie Brothers distillery dating back to the
1880s. This is also a popular watering hole as they
offer over 160 whiskeys and over 100 bourbons and
have an excellent wine list. Menu favorites include

Doc Chicken, Half Slab of Ribs, oysters on the half shell with bourbon mignonette and Carolina pulled pork.

THE EAGLE

1314 Bardstown Rd, Louisville, 502-498-8420
https://www.eaglerestaurant.com/
CUISINE: Southern/American (Traditional)
DRINKS: Full Bar
SERVING: Lunch & Dinner
PRICE RANGE: $$
NEIGHBORHOOD: Cherokee Triangle
Fun eatery featuring a lot of wooden accents in the interior and a big eagle painting on the brick wall. Lively bar scene with several beers on draft. Expansive outdoor area with seating at large picnic tables. Menu carries Southern classics and comfort food. Known for their Fried Chicken, which you can order in quarters (choose white or dark meat), a half chicken or a whole. (They serve the chicken with a spicy hot honey concoction I'd never tasted before.) One of their appetizers is a sausage & kale dip that's interesting. Sides include spoonbread (a great dish I rarely see these days), white cheddar grits, and delicious mashed potatoes with a little horseradish whipped into it that gives it a delightful kick topped off with a savory gravy. Their homemade biscuits are served with a great blackberry jam and honey butter. Good selection of sandwiches and salads as well. (And they're all very good quality, not just a perfunctory nod to the menu category.)

ENGLISH GRILL
BROWN HOTEL
335 W Broadway, Louisville, 502-583-1234
www.brownhotel.com
This is the home of the original "Hot Brown," a sort of "baked sandwich," made with roasted turkey and toast points with a layer of Mornay sauce slopped over it all and topped with pecorino Romano cheese and bacon and tomatoes. People loved this concoction when it was first introduced in the 1920s and they've kept coming back for more. Of course, you can get this Louisville favorite in restaurants all over town, but it makes for a good story to tell your friends you ate it in the place where it was invented. When I'm here, however, I don't eat the Hot Brown (it's too filling for me). I go for the seared scallop Benedict (lamb bacon, quail egg and Béarnaise); or the crispy pork belly, served with Maker's Mark salted caramel candied apple and a Dijon trotter galette. The Hot

Brown shouldn't overshadow the other great cuisine served here. This is one of the top 10 restaurants in town. Not the most *fun,* but certainly the best.

FEAST BBQ

909 E Market St, Ste 100, Louisville, 502-749-9900
www.feastbbq.com
CUISINE: Barbeque/American (Traditional)
DRINKS: Full Bar
SERVING: Lunch, Dinner
PRICE RANGE: $$
NEIGHBORHOOD: NuLu
Quaint little BBQ spot located in a former truck repair shop. Order up front and pay, then seat yourself at a picnic table while you wait for your order. Simple menu of BBQ, sides and drinks. Try the Country Boy Brewing Cougar Bait Ale, just one of the many local beers on tap. The weekends find this place packed with locals who come from miles around. Family friendly.

GARAGE BAR

700 E Market St, Louisville, 502-749-7100
www.garageonmarket.com
CUISINE: Pizza and more
DRINKS: Full Bar
SERVING: Dinner 7 nights; lunch on weekends
PRICE RANGE: $$
NEIGHBORHOOD: NuLu

The brick oven pizzas are the main attraction here. I should say "gourmet pizzas." The brick oven comes from Italy. Half the battle with pizza is won with the crust. They make their own here, using fresh yeast. They have their own "milled tomato" sauce, and that's the other half of the battle. Nice snacks like "rolled oysters," pork meatballs, boiled peanuts (a Southern tradition) and cauliflower salad. The country ham comes on a charcuterie board or on a pizza. The bar stocks some 25 to 30 specialty beers and a huge variety of rye and bourbon whiskeys from Kentucky.

GRIND BURGER KITCHEN

829 E. Market, Louisville, 502-213-0277
www.grindburgerkitchen.com
CUISINE: Burgers, Vegetarian
DRINKS: No Booze
SERVING: Lunch & dinner, Tues-Fri.
PRICE RANGE: $$
NEIGHBORHOOD: Preston

Liz and Jesse had run Louisville's favorite burger truck that traveled through the neighborhoods serving up some of the best hamburgers in the city made from local, grass-fed beef. The truck is gone, replaced with this brick-and-mortar eatery. You'll want to order the burger with 2 slices of Brie, thick-cut bacon and their special habanero jam that gives the thing a kick. Don't forget the essential side of fries.

HAMMERHEAD'S

921 Swan St, Louisville, 502-365-1112
www.louisvillehammerheads.com
CUISINE: Southern/American
DRINKS: Beer
SERVING: Dinner; closed Sundays
PRICE RANGE: $$
Small unique eatery offering a menu of pub grub including smoked meats (they use a double-barreled smoker for most of the meats served here), and vegetarian options. I'd get the "PBLT," which is a pork BLT, with generous cuts of smoked pork providing the delicious difference. Great variety of

creatively conceived burgers, which explains why the lines start forming before they open at 5. No reservations, so get there early or go on a weekday.

JACK FRY'S

1007 Bardstown Rd, Louisville, 502-452-9244
www.jackfrys.com
CUISINE: American
DRINKS: Full Bar
SERVING: Breakfast, Lunch, Dinner
PRICE RANGE: $$$
NEIGHBORHOOD: Highlands- Cherokee Triangle
Some come for the music, others the food, and both
deserve raves. This joint opened in 1933 and you'll
wonder if they've ever renovated. It's got a warm Old
South feel to it. You'll want to browse all the photos
from the 1930s that decorate the walls. There are
photos of the 1937 flood that swamped downtown. It
was the damage done by this flood that instigated the
development of the eastern parts of town that are now
among the most upscale. The Southern inspired menu
features favorites like beef filet, and scallops and
winter melon. Great desserts like the Hazelnut torte.
Live music every night (usually a piano player) with
jazz on Monday, Friday & Saturday.

MAYAN CAFÉ

813 E Market St, Louisville, 502-566-0651
www.themayancafe.com
CUISINE: Mayan
DRINKS: Full Bar
SERVING: Lunch & Dinner weekdays; dinner
only Saturday; closed Sunday
PRICE RANGE: $$
NEIGHBORHOOD: NuLu
Chef Bruce Ucan is from the Yucatan Peninsula, so he
knows what's original and what's fake. Still, he adds a
lot of twists to traditional Mexican fare in this simple
and unpretentious place. Dishes like black bean cakes;
empanadas with chorizo, mozzarella and tomato-
habanero sauce; oven -roasted rabbit with pumpkin
seed mole and fried plantains; a burger made with
grass-fed beef, bolillo bread, greens, pickled onions,
tomatoes and Havarti cheese; *cochinita pibil*, or
roasted pork. Flatbreads are served at lunch. There are
numerous vegetarian dishes.

MUSSEL & BURGER BAR

113 South 7th St, Louisville, 502-749-6451
9200 Taylorsville Rd, Louisville, 502-384-4834
https://www.mussel-burger-bar.com/
CUISINE: Mussels / Burgers / American
(Traditional)
DRINKS: Full Bar
SERVING: Lunch & Dinner
PRICE RANGE: $$
NEIGHBORHOOD: 2 locations – Downtown & East
End
Popular bistro with a vintage décor and lots of wood,
from the ceiling to the floor to the chairs to the big
wooden back-bar, relieved a little by the banquettes
and the slender white columns painted a stark white
to offer some contrast against the otherwise dark
interior. Has a very different menu of American fare
with some nods to Europe. While the different
offerings of mussels are certainly a draw (get them
served as Moules Basquaise (with chorizo, olive oil,
lobster broth), Greek style, Meuniere (white wine,
shallots, garlic, butter), Curry Cream, Blue Cheese
Beer or Mexican Pozole), the great selection of
burgers (probably 14 to 16 creative iterations) almost
certainly draws an even larger crowd of patrons.
Favorites: Blue Cheese Beer Mussels; Spanish Blue
Burger (La Peral Spanish blue cheese & fig
marmalade). They also serve a variety of salads;
sandwiches and the sides bear a close look. Great
cocktails.

PROOF ON MAIN
21C MUSEUM HOTEL
702 West Main St, Louisville, 502-217-6360
www.proofonmain.com
CUISINE: Contemporary American
DRINKS: Full Bar
SERVING: Breakfast, Lunch & Dinner
PRICE RANGE: $$$$
NEIGHBORHOOD: Downtown
I already wrote about what a fabulous environment
this place enjoys because it's located in the 21c
Museum Hotel. Charred octopus; garlic risotto;
Woodland Farm's hog chop; scallops served with
corn bread, country ham, asparagus, gremolata and
sorghum; bison burger with smoked bacon and
Tillamook cheddar. For something different, try the
Kentucky trout tartare. Almost everything served here
is locally sourced. The bar's a great place to hang out.

Both places are bright airy rooms with lots of art decorating the walls.

ROYALS HOT CHICKEN

736 E Market St, Louisville, 502-919-7068
www.royalschicken.com/
CUISINE: American Traditional
DRINKS: Full bar
SERVING: Lunch & Dinner; closed Sunday
PRICE RANGE: $$
NEIGHBORHOOD: NuLu
Known for their great Nashville Hot Fried Chicken.
Modern, spacious eatery with a creative menu of
traditional American fare. Nice selection of beers and
delicious creative shakes (try the bourbon shake).
Counter service.

THE SILVER DOLLAR

1761 Frankfort Ave, Louisville, (502) 259-9540
www.whiskeybythedrink.com
CUISINE: Gastropub, Southern
DRINKS: Full Bar
SERVING: Brunch, Dinner, Late night
PRICE RANGE: $$
NEIGHBORHOOD: Crescent Hills
This gastropub located in a former red brick firehouse
is a celebration of an old 1950s Bakersfield,
California, honky-tonk serving great Southern dishes
like Chicken Fried Steak, Breaded Catfish, and Fried
Chicken Livers. The bar serves Kentucky bourbon
and rye whiskeys and is home to some interesting
craft cocktails. There's also an incredible list of beers.

TACO LUCHADOR

938 Baxter Ave, Louisville, 502-583-0440
5202 New Cut Rd, Louisville, 502-384-8457
9204 Taylorsville Rd, Louisville, 502-708-1675
112 Meridian Av, Louisville, 502-709-
5154 https://www.el-taco-luchador.com/
CUISINE: Tacos
DRINKS: Full Bar
SERVING: Lunch & Dinner
PRICE RANGE: $$
NEIGHBORHOOD: several locations
I love the startling yellow bar seats here in this small
Mexican joint. They and their yellow table chair
counterparts are that Mexican color used by
Fiestaware in the 1960s. (They are blue in a different
location.) Plenty of outdoor seating as well. Counter

eatery serving tacos, tortas, nachos, and sandwiches, all very high quality. Frozen margaritas.

WAGNER'S PHARMACY

3113 S Fourth St, Louisville, 502-375-3800
www.wagnerspharmacy.com
CUISINE: American, Burgers
DRINKS: No Booze
SERVING: Breakfast, Brunch
PRICE RANGE: $$
NEIGHBORHOOD: South Louisville
This is a shrine for those who love the Kentucky Derby with horse racing memorabilia pasted all over the walls. When you walk in here, it's like walking through a time machine because the place doesn't look like it's changed much since it opened in 1922. It's a pharmacy with an all-American diner serving burgers and such. It's not the food that's the attraction. Go the day after the Derby and meet the trainers and jockeys that lost the race the day before. Since it's located right outside Churchill Downs, the place is always crawling with trainers, jockeys, groomsmen, track workers and betters. Be sure to look over the photos of past legends who used to frequent the place.

WILD EGGS

121 S Floyd St, Louisville, 502-690-5925
153 English Station Rd, Louisville, 502-618-3449
1311 Herr Lane, Louisville, 502-618-2905
3985 Dutchmans Lane, Louisville, 502-893-8005
https://wildeggs.com/
CUISINE: Breakfast/American (New)

DRINKS: No Booze
SERVING: Breakfast & Lunch
PRICE RANGE: $$
NEIGHBORHOOD: several locations
This may be a "chain" restaurant, but they succeed in bringing the high quality and creative attention to details to a simple-enough breakfast-focused concept that you expect to find when you go to a "fine dining" restaurant. The staff is smart & friendly (as opposed to dull-witted & surly you often find in so many breakfast-only joints) and the food of the highest quality, from the fresh-squeezed orange juice to the homemade cinnamon bun (with croissant style bread stuffed with butter, brown sugar & cinnamon, cooked in a cast iron skillet and topped with sweet vanilla bean icing). While the focus is on breakfast (with crepes, omelets, several Benedict selections, pancakes, waffles, French toast), they also have high quality sandwiches, salads and soups. Favorites: Sweet Home Apple Bourbon Crepes; Chicken crepes with a side of pancakes; Build Your Own Omelet (with a wide selection of fillings); Jimmy the Greek Frittata; the Hash Brown Casserole is a side dish you'll go nuts over.

WILTSHIRE BAKERY & CAFE

901 Barret Ave, Louisville, 502-581-8560
www.wiltshirepantry.com/bakery-and-cafe
CUISINE: Breakfast/Brunch
DRINKS: Beer & Wine Only
SERVING: Breakfast & Lunch; closed Mondays
PRICE RANGE: $

The black-and-white chalkboard menu gives this combination bakery and café offering a great bakery counter with a wide selection of pastries, artisanal breads and brioche a homey, small-town feeling. Café offers breakfast and light lunch fare. They have a homemade "fried apple pie," kind of their take on a Pop Tart, but in much better flavors. Or get their Croque Monsieur with savory ham and melted Gruyere cheese served atop their homemade brioche.

WILTSHIRE ON MARKET

636 E Market St, Louisville, 502-589-5224
www.wiltshirepantry.com
CUISINE: American (New)
DRINKS: Full Bar
SERVING: Dinner; Thurs - Sun
PRICE RANGE: $$
Popular eatery offering a great dining experience and top-notch cocktails. Creative menu includes dishes like: Smoked Alligator Tacos and Beef Pave & potato onion cakes. Expansive cocktail menu.

YUMMY POLLO

4222-B Bishop Lane, Louisville, 502-618-1400
http://yummypollo.com/
CUISINE: Peruvian/Latin American
DRINKS: No Booze
SERVING: Lunch & Dinner, Closed on Sunday
PRICE RANGE: $
NEIGHBORHOOD: Hayfield Dundee
Very basic Peruvian eatery where chicken is the king (their slogan). Peruvian style charcoal fired rotisserie chicken is their specialty. (High quality naturally

raised hormone-free chickens.) That and their tasty side dishes (get their cilantro lime rice) is all there is to it, but it's more finger-licking good than "You Know Where." Order at counter and eat at one of the handful of tables provided or get it to go. Outdoor seating is nothing to brag about. You're sitting on the sidewalk next to the parking lot. No, the décor is nothing. The food everything. And it's cheap.

Chapter 5

NIGHTLIFE

BARDSTOWN ROAD

Down the 2-mile-long Bardstown – Baxter Avenue Corridor there are something like 40 bars, some of then located in dumpy little dives and others in fancy upscale restaurants. But it's the best place to spend an evening bar hopping. Besides the bars, you'll find a captivating collection of galleries, shops, antique stores, artisans selling crafts and tourist traps selling cheap merchandise. But it's great fun.

3RD ST. DIVE

442 S 3rd St, Louisville, 502-749-3483
www.reverbnation.com/venue/thirdstreetdive
NEIGHBORHOOD: Fourth Street, Downtown
Once a haven for punk rockers, this dive bar now offers a variety including Rock, Rockabilly, Honky

Tonk, Country, Blues, and Jazz. Filled with local art –
that's for sale. Happy hour specials. Theme nights,
karaoke, darts, and pool.

BACK DOOR
1250 Bardstown Rd, Louisville, 502-451-0659
www.thebackdoorlouisville.com
NEIGHBORHOOD: Highlands - Tyler Park,
Bardstown Road
Serving cocktails for over twenty-five years, this late-
night neighborhood bar lives up to its motto "Bikers
to brain surgeons." No pretense here, just friendly
service. Simple cocktails. Menu of bar snacks. Lots of
pool tables.

BROWNIES
9900 Linn Station Rd, Louisville, 502-326-9830
www.browniestheshed.com
NEIGHBORHOOD: Plainview Family-owned
Sports Bar. Simple pub-grub menu. Outdoor patio
open during warm weather.

CHECKS
1101 E Burnett Ave, Louisville, 502-637-9515
www.checkscafelouisville.com
NEIGHBORHOOD: Schnitzelburg German-
American restaurant/bar serving beer, sandwiches
and classic German fare. Known for their burgers.
Happy hour daily. Lengthy beer list. Live music.
Lots of TVs for sports.

HIGH HORSE

1032 Story Ave, Louisville, 502-690-5020
www.highhorsebar.com
NEIGHBORHOOD: Butchertown
Cozy neighborhood bar with booths and bar seating.
Small menu of bar grub. Arcade games. Local crowd.

HOLY GRALE

1034 Bardstown Rd, Louisville, 502-857-7457
www.thegrales.com/
NEIGHBORHOOD: Bardstown Road / Highlands

Formerly a Unitarian Church dating back to 1905, this dark and cozy Victorian structure in the Highlands neighborhood is now a gathering place for those who worship the international beers (some of them quite rare) served at Holy Grale. The bar features over 25 taps and an impressive bottle list. The bar menu is good, with things like Pork Belly Sliders and Chorizo Tacos. Try to run up to the loft where the choir used to sing just so you can see the original stained-glass windows.

MAGNOLIA BAR & GRILL

1398 S 2nd St, Louisville, 502-637-9052
www.magbarlouisville.com
This popular dive bar fills up for late night action. The name "grill" is misleading as no food is served here. There is a small concert stage however, the music is generally provided by a jukebox or a DJ playing EDM music on Wednesday nights, when drinks are even cheaper. (Sunday they do a Bingo Night.)

MERRYWEATHER

1101 Lydia St, Louisville, No Phone
www.themerryweather.net/
NEIGHBORHOOD: Schnitzelburg
Friendly locals' hangout with a long bar, booths, a small stage, and a room with pinball machines. TVs play a non-stop reel of women go-go dancers. Local beers on tap, nice selection of canned and bottled beers. Menu of small bites.

META

425 W Chestnut St, Louisville, 502-822-6382
www.metalouisville.com
Located in downtown Louisville, this upscale
speakeasy-themed bar specializes in craft and classic
cocktails in an atmosphere that takes you back in
time: penny-tiled floors, hand painted wallpaper.
Speaking of "classic," if you've never had the classic
Sidecar, you'll get a good one here.

NOWHERE BAR

1133 Bardstown Rd, Louisville, 502-552-6942
www.nowherelouisville.com
Gay video and dance bar that pumps electronic dance
music all night. If you're not into dancing there's lots
of TVs, pool tables and an outdoor patio. Many theme
nights with DJs, karaoke, and trivia.

OLD LOUISVILLE TAVERN

1532 S 4th St, Louisville, 502-409-6281
www.oldlouisvilletavern.com
NEIGHBORHOOD: Old Louisville

Neighborhood tavern/hangout popular among locals. Local brews on tap. Theme nights (Margarita & Tequila night is Tuesday). Menu features specialty burgers and comfort food. Outdoor patio open weather permitting.

OLD SEELBACH BAR
SEELBACH HILTON HOTEL
500 Fourth Ave, Louisville, 502-585-3200
www.seelbachhilton.com
You must stop in here for a drink. Just one at least, if only to walk through the majestic lobby of this grand hotel with its marble columns, coffered ceilings and rich wood finishes. Scott Fitzgerald, before he wrote "The Great Gatsby," used to hang out in this bar when he was stationed in Louisville as a second lieutenant. Fitzgerald long ago drank himself into oblivion, but you're still here. Why not try a "bourbon tasting"? You get 4 one-ounce pours for about $20.

OUTLOOK INN
916 Baxter Ave, Louisville, 502-583-4661
No Website
NEIGHBORHOOD: Original Highlands
Relaxed hangout offering great cocktails, nice music, and friendly service. Bartenders play games in between serving beers. Impressive list of bourbons and craft beers.

THE PEARL
1151 Goss Ave, Louisville, 502-996-7552
No Website
NEIGHBORHOOD: Germantown
Funky local's tavern with a retro feel. Casual happy hour. Impressive selection of private single barrel bourbons. Bar games and old-school music. Theme nights.

PINTS & UNION
114 E Market St, New Albany, 812-725-0081
www.pintsandunion.com
NEIGHBORHOOD: New Albany
Cozy public house with a great selection of beers and well stocked bar. Menu of small plates and burgers. Outdoor patio. Board games on the second floor.

THE SILVER DOLLAR

1761 Frankfort Ave, Louisville, 502-259-9540
www.whiskeybythedrink.com
NEIGHBORHOOD: Crescent Hills
A great hangout for the bourbon and whiskey
connoisseur. This former fire house with its red brick
walls makes a good place to enjoy the 100-odd
whiskeys on offer. They have a large collection of
vinyl and play music from the likes of Merle Haggard
and other country rock singers from the 1950s that
personified the Bakersfield sound.

TAJ

807 E Market St, Louisville, 877-825-6858
NO WEBSITE
NEIGHBORHOOD: NuLu
Relaxed offbeat dive bar serving up bourbon and
bourbon-based cocktails. Nice beer selection. Seating
at the bar or tables. Outdoor patio.

ZANZABAR

2100 South Preston St, Louisville, 502-635-9227
www.zanzabarlouisville.com
NEIGHBORHOOD: Schnitzelburg
This is a small music venue and dive bar but it's also
a full-service restaurant serving Southern cuisine.
Live music schedule features everything from
traveling punk bands to popular Louisville bands. The
food is good and they even have some great vintage
video games.

Chapter 6

WHAT TO SEE & DO

ACTORS THEATER OF LOUISVILLE
316 West Main St, Louisville, 502) 536-8944 www.actorstheatre.org
This theatre is recognized nationally for its achievements in the arts and critically acclaimed productions. The company presents original and classic theater works. Plays that premiere here go on to tour the world. Pulitzer Prizes have been awarded to "dinner with Friends" and "Crimes of the Heart," both of which originated here. The **Humana Festival of New American Plays** runs in the spring.

BIG FOUR BRIDGE 1101
River Rd., Louisville,
502-574-3768
https://ourwaterfront.org/
HOURS: 6 a.m. – 11 p.m.
ADMISSION: No fee

NEIGHBORHOOD: Downtown/Waterfront

The Big Four Bridge is a six-span former railroad truss bridge that crosses the Ohio River, connecting Louisville with Jeffersonville in Indiana. It was completed in 1895 and updated in 1929. You can walk across it in 10 minutes.

BUFFALO TRACE DISTILLERY

113 Great Buffalo Trace, Frankfort, 866-729-3722
www.buffalotracedistillery.com
HOURS: 9 – 5; Thurs – Sat.
ADMISSION: No fee

Popular for tourists and locals, the tour begins with a video and then winds through a path of rolling bourbon barrels offering a behind-the-scenes peek at a distillery in action. Visitors get to taste some of the award-winning products. Reservations only needed for large groups. Tours last approximately 1 hour.

CAVE HILL CEMETERY

701 Baxter Ave, Louisville, 502-451-5630
www.cavehillcemetery.com
Col. Harlan Sanders of Kentucky Fried Chicken fame
is buried here. So is George Rogers Clark, who
founded Louisville. (He was the brother of William
Clark, who formed the Clark part of the Lewis &
Clark Expedition.) Tours are available. This 296-acre
Victorian era National Cemetery and arboretum are
open daily. The stunning landscaping and massive
trees are just as impressive as the marble and granite
headstones. Whether you're a Civil War buff or a
garden enthusiast, this is must-see. Over 5,000
soldiers are buried here, many dating back to the Civil
War. Listed on the National Register of Historic
Places, this is the largest cemetery in the area. The
cemetery is the site of natural rock outcroppings and
hilly topography and features ponds, statuary, and
architecturally elegant tombs. The cemetery boasts
more than 500 kinds of trees and garden plants
growing in the gardens that you will find it a beautiful
getaway from the busy Highlands neighborhood
nearby.

CHEROKEE PARK

745 Cochran Hill Rd, Louisville, 502-574-7275
https://louisvilleky.gov/government/parks/park-list/cherokee-park
Designed in 1891 by Frederick Law Olmsted (some people consider the work he did in Louisville to be even greater than his work on Central Park or Brooklyn's Prospect Park), this 409-acre park is listed as the 69th most popular municipal park in the country. Beargrass Creek runs though the park, crossed by many pedestrian and automobile bridges. Park features include: a 2.4-mile scenic loop with separate lanes for traffic and bikes.

CHURCHILL DOWNS

700 Central Ave, Louisville, 502-636-4400
www.churchilldowns.com
This racetrack is known worldwide as the annual host
for 3-year-old thoroughbreds running in the Kentucky
Derby. If you don't want to put up with the insane
crowds on Derby Day, attend one of the other race
days when there is no hassle. You'll get to roam
around the storied track for a small fee. In the lobby
there's the **Kentucky Derby Museum**, which is a lot
of fun. (This track officially opened in 1875, the same
year as the first Kentucky Derby.) This track is rated
the 5th in America and has a capacity of 120,000
people.

COPPER & KINGS

1121 E Washington St, Louisville, 502-561-0267
http://www.copperandkings.com/
HOURS: 10 a.m. – 4 p.m.

ADMISSION: Minimal fee
NEIGHBORHOOD: Butchertown
Distillery that crafts untraditional distilled Pure Pot-still brandies. Tours offered 10 a.m. – 3 p.m. on the hours. Thurs – Mon. Rooftop tasting with breathtaking view of Louisville skyline. Reservations recommended.

EVAN WILLIAMS BOURBON EXPERIENCE

528 W Main St, Louisville, 502-272-2623
http://evanwilliams.com/visit.php
HOURS: Open daily
ADMISSION: Minimal admission fee
NEIGHBORHOOD: Downtown/West Main Located on Louisville's historic "Whiskey Row" featuring an artisanal distillery, guided tours, and educational Bourbon tastings (if you can call it that!). Learn the history of Kentucky's first commercial distiller and the history of Kentucky's native spirit.

FALLS OF THE OHIO

201 W Riverside Dr, Clarksville, 812-280-9970
www.fallsoftheohio.org/
HOURS: 7 a.m. – 11 p.m.
ADMISSION: Nominal fee plus parking
NEIGHBORHOOD: Ohio River
Located on the banks of the Ohio River, this State Park is home to 390-million-year-old fossil beds. Park activities include fishing, hiking, walking, fossil viewing, bird watching, and picnicking.

KENTUCKY CENTER FOR THE ARTS

501 West Main St, Louisville, 502-584-7777
www.kentuckycenter.org
This Center houses some of the city's major arts
organizations and offers an impressive roster of
music, dance, theater and other events. Home to The
**Louisville Orchestra, Kentucky Opera, Louisville
Ballet, Stage One** and PNC Bank Broadway Across
America.

KENTUCKY DERBY MUSEUM

704 Central Ave, Louisville, 502-637-1111
www.derbymuseum.org
My first time in Louisville was not to attend the Derby.
But my first stop when I got settled was still Churchill
Downs because of this museum. Located on the front
steps of historic Churchill Downs, this museum is one
of Louisville's premiere attractions. Here you can learn
all about the Kentucky Derby any time during the year.
The two-level museum features exhibits that celebrate
thoroughbred racing and the Kentucky Derby – known
as the first jewel in racing's Triple Crown. Here you can
mount a fake horse and "ride it" for the same 2 minutes
it takes to run in the Derby. There's also a hi-def film
shown in on a 360-degree screen that takes you through
the history of the Derby, which was first run here in
1785, the year the track first opened. Take one of the
"backside" tours to the barn areas where a thousand
horses live during the racing meet. When there is no
racing, other tours take you into Churchill Downs and
you get to go to places casual visitors never see.

LOUISVILLE GLASSWORKS

815 West Market St, Louisville, 502-515-2489
www.louisvilleglassworks.com
This unique center of glassworks offers what they like
to label as "edutainment" opportunities. Visitors get

to enjoy the walk-in workshop, tours, flameworking experiences and the gallery that exhibits flameworked glass, flat glass and jewelry fashioned by some 30 artists. Glassworks facilities include: a hot shop, a welding shop, a glass gallery and a gift shop. The newest addition is the "Flame Your Own Snowman" workshop where guests can work with artist Mark Payton to create their own snowman. Daily tours available for a nominal fee.

LOUISVILLE HISTORIC TOURS

Corner South 4th Street &, W Ormsby Ave, Louisville, 502-718-2764
http://louisvillehistorictours.com/
HOURS: 11 a.m. – 9:30 p.m. daily.
ADMISSION: Modest fee ($20 pp)
NEIGHBORHOOD: Old Louisville
These 90 – minute walking tours are led by a knowledgeable tour guide through the streets of Louisville passing a variety of historic homes, big and small, from Victorian style to Romanesque. Reservations recommended.

LOUISVILLE SLUGGER MUSEUM

800 West Main St, Louisville, 877-775-8443
www.sluggermuse um.com
You can't miss the 120-foot-high baseball bat outside this place on Main Street. You can visit the main lobby for free. In this lobby is the **Signature Wall**, where you'll find 8,000-plus signatures of players who signed contracts to use the famous bat. If you pay admission to the museum, you get a tour of the factory where bats are made that are used by many

Major League players. (You'll smell the maple and white ash woods used to make the bats.) And, handle bats once used by Cal Ripken, Jr., and Mickey Mantle. (For a fee, they'll even make a bat with your name on it as a souvenir.) Outside is the **Louisville Slugger Walk of Fame**, which runs a mile from the museum down to the city's minor-league ballpark. You'll pass by bronze monuments and plaques documenting such baseball greats as Ty Cobb and Babe Ruth. I love baseball, so this is all great fun for me.

MINT JULEP TOURS

502-583-1433

www.mintjuleptours.com

They offer a Bourbon Trail Tour that takes you out to the distilleries to see how bourbon is made first-hand. But they also offer Louisville city tours (the city's only real comprehensive tour), horse country tours and culinary tours.

MUHAMMAD ALI CENTER

144 North Sixth St, Louisville, 502-584-9254

https://alicenter.org

The Center offers three levels of award-winning exhibitions and galleries celebrating the life and career of Muhammad Ali. The museum features many interactive and multimedia exhibits. (Go ahead and try your hand at the speed bag.) The Center is also known for its programming that serves people of all cultures, ages, nationalities, and geographic areas.

MUSEUM ROW ON MAIN

Main St, Louisville

https://museumrowlouisville.com/

Museum Row consists of nine original galleries or museums located within four walkable blocks on Main Street. The venues include: 21C Museum Hotel, Frazier History Museum, Glassworks, Kentucky Center for the Performing Arts, Kentucky Museum of Art & Craft, Kentucky Show!, Louisville Science Center, Louisville Slugger Museum & Factory, and Muhammad Ali Center. Check website for events.

OHIO RIVER

Thomas Jefferson called the Ohio River "the most beautiful river on earth." This river marks Kentucky's northern border and the normally gentle river breaks its smooth run with the Falls of the Ohio, a 2.2-mile-long limestone rapids. Here the river drops 23.9 feet.

OLD LOUISVILLE

North of the University of Louisville main campus is the section of town called Old Louisville, and it runs to the southern border of downtown. Expect to see lots of stately Victorian homes tucked in on both sides of gorgeous tree-lined streets. Where once the elite lived in the 19th Century, like a lot of such sections, the 20th Century was not kind to it and it became rundown and awful, but gentrification has brought it back big-time. Well worth the time.

SPEED ART MUSEUM

2035 S 3rd St, Louisville, 502-634-2700
www.speedmuseum.org/
HOURS: 10 a.m. – 5 p.m.; Noon – 5 p.m. on Sun; Closed Mondays
ADMISSION: Nominal fee
NEIGHBORHOOD: University
Originally known as the J.B. Speed Memorial Museum, this is the oldest, largest, and most acclaimed museum of art in Kentucky. Museum offers modern architecture, inventive programming, interactive exhibits, and a variety of "art experiences." Museum offers weekly events, the Speed Concert Series, an Interactive Family gallery, and a popular late-night event called Art After Dark. Museum houses a collection of African art, ancient art, Native American art, American art, European art, and contemporary art. Arts represented include Rembrandt, Rubens, Monet, Rodin, Gainsborough, Picasso, Cezanne, Matisse, and modern works by artists such as Chuck Close and Frank Stella.

SWANSON CONTEMPORARY

638 East Market St, Louisville, 502-589-5466
www.swansoncontemporary.com
Located in the East Market Gallery District (now called "**NuLu**," for "New Louisville"), which has been gentrified and is now filled with interesting places, this being one of them: a gallery that showcases contemporary national and regional artists focusing on works in video, installation, photography, conceptual art, painting, performance, and sculpture. This gallery mounts ten exhibitions annually on the main level with a lower-level video and installation space and outdoor sculpture garden.

WHISKEY ROW

This is a block-long stretch from 101-133 W. Main Street that once served as home to the bourbon industry in Louisville, Kentucky. The collection of Revivalist and Chicago School-style buildings with cast-iron storefronts were built between 1852 and 1905. On a list of Louisville Most Endangered Historic Places, the buildings were slated for demolition in 2011, but some quick-thinking people worked up an agreement among the city, local developers, and preservationists that saved Whiskey Row.

WATERFRONT PARK

River Rd, Louisville, 502-574-3768
https://ourwaterfront.org/
Popular 85-acre park adjacent to downtown Louisville and the Ohio River. Landscaped for optimum usage with paths for running and biking. Lots of family activities. Equipped with picnic tables, benches, and playgrounds, a lot of this park overlooks the Ohio River, giving it an added dimension. The

park's Great Lawn is like a massive front yard for the city and is site of many events including Thunder Over Louisville, Derby Festival and Forecastle Festival. Here you'll also find the **Big Four Bridge**, a former railroad bridge connecting Louisville and Jeffersonville, Ind., that was redesigned as a pedestrian walkway and cycling route.

ZEPHYR GALLERY

610 East Market St, Louisville, 502-585-5646
www.zephyrgallery.org
This multidisciplinary exhibition space is an artist-run initiative that offers proposal-based exhibitions and collaborations.

2981260
BOURBON WHISKEY
RC-53-G   DSP-KY-31
SERIAL NO. 87 109
2981260

Chapter 7
SHOPPING & SERVICES

CARMICHAEL'S BOOKSTORE

1295 Bardstown Rd, Louisville, 502-456-6950
www.carmichaelsbookstore.com
This is Louisville's oldest indie bookstore featuring shelf after shelf of new and old titles. Visit the website for a schedule of upcoming events and book signings, authors' readings, etc.

CITY CONCIERGE

502-836-4376
www.cityconciergelouisville.com

Online personal concierge service that is tailored to each clients needs and interests. Get information and access for nightclubs and local events. Tips o shopping, services, galleries, and shopping.

COLLECTIONS

Westport Village, 1301 Herr Ln # 181, Louisville, 502-749-7200
https://shopcollectionscloset.com **WEBSITE DOWN AT PRESSTIME**
Collections, a locally run fashion boutique, provides a variety of fashions for women of all ages. The boutique features everything from handbags to shoes, faux leather slacks, snazzy party dresses and lots more. It may be located in a strip mall, but don't let that put you off. Lots of treasures inside this place.

FOURTH STREET LIVE

411 S 4th St, Louisville, 502-584-7170
www.4thstlive.com

This is an urban mall with a variety of stores and restaurants. Restaurants include: T.G.I. Fridays, Hard Rock Café, and RiRa Irish Pub. Nightlife venues include: PBR Louisville A Cowboy Bar, The Marquee Bar, Kill Devil Club and Howl at the Moon. The food court also has chain restaurants like Philly Station, Wendy's, Subway, KFC, and Taco Bell. Retail outlets include CVS, Foot Locker, and T-Mobile.

HEINE BROTHERS' COFFEE
1250 Bardstown Rd, Louisville, 502-456-5108
www.heinebroscoffee.com
Heine Brothers has great coffee. This is a great place to have a seat outside after you've bought a book at **Carmichael's** just adjacent. **SEVERAL LOCATIONS IN THE LOUISVILLE AREA.**

PLEASE & THANK YOU

800 E Market St, Louisville, 502-533-0113
www.pleaseandthankyoulouisville.com
NEIGHBORHOOD: NuLu
A bakery that has such popular chocolate chip cookies that they created a "baking kit" so you can make them at home. (They won't reveal the exact recipe.) Great coffees, bagels, scones, brownies, other baked goods. Good coffees and teas. They have great paninis: a breakfast version made with local eggs, basil pesto, mozzarella on focaccia; there's also cinnamon toast, a brioche topped with butter, cinnamon and sugar. Oh, God, does that take me back to my youth. Peanut butter toast, too.

REVELRY BOUTIQUE GALLERY

742 E Market St, Louisville, 502-414-1278
www.revelrygallery.com/

Beautiful shop filled with revolving selection of handmade goods curated by the owner. A super selection of jewelry, home décor, art, home goods, and other creative items made by local artisans.

RODES

4938 Brownsboro Rd, Louisville, 502-753-7633
www.rodes.com
NEIGHBORHOOD: Brownsboro
Since 1914, this has been a popular shopping destination offering the best men's and women's apparel. Get a seersucker suit and a Panama hat. The men's shop has two in-shop boutiques featuring Ermenegildo Zegna and Eton of Sweden collections. For the ladies, there's an eclectic selection of designer fashions including shoes, handbags, jewelry, scarves, and skin care products. (And they have a big selection of hats you'll need for Derby Day.)

SCOUT

3626 Brownsboro Rd., Louisville, 502-584-8989
www.scoutonmarket.com/
NEIGHBORHOOD: NuLu
Small home accessories and giftware shop sporting
an eclectic mix of furniture, home goods, accessories,
art, jewelry, and one-of-a-kind gifts. Shop also
features select men's clothing items, books, cards,
and knick-knacks.

<u>INDEX</u>